Lettering THE ALPHABET

IN 30 WAYS

HAND LETTERING & CALLIGRAPHY ALPHABETS

EMAIL US AT

hellosimplepress@gmail.com

 **to get free extras!**

Just title the email "Lettered Goods"

And we will send some extra surprises your way!

Learn simple ways to create new lettering styles with the tips and inspiration you'll find on the following pages!!

Remember to always start in pencil and...

CREATING Variation

LETTERFORM:

This is the shape and style of a letter. Between uppercase and lowercase letters, the variations are endless!

A d A A

↓

STROKE:

These are the lines that create the letterform. Alter the thickness of your lines to create the traditional calligraphy and hand lettering look.

A A A A

↓

SERIFS:

You can further create variation by adding different details, called serifs, to the end of your strokes.

A A A A

A *A* *A* *a* *A* *A* *A* *A* *A* *A*

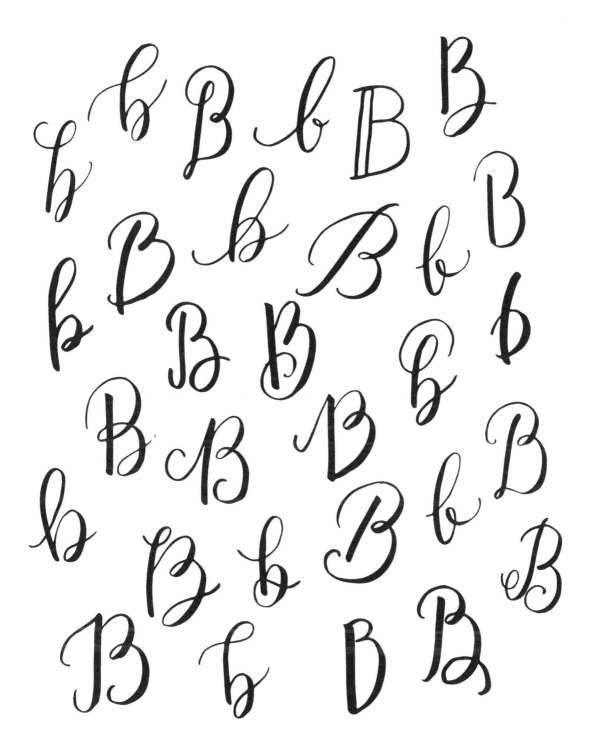

$\mathcal{C}$

$\mathcal{C}$

$\mathcal{C}$

$\mathcal{C}$

$\mathcal{x}$

$\mathcal{C}$

$\mathcal{C}$

$\mathcal{C}$

$\mathcal{C}$

$\mathcal{v}$

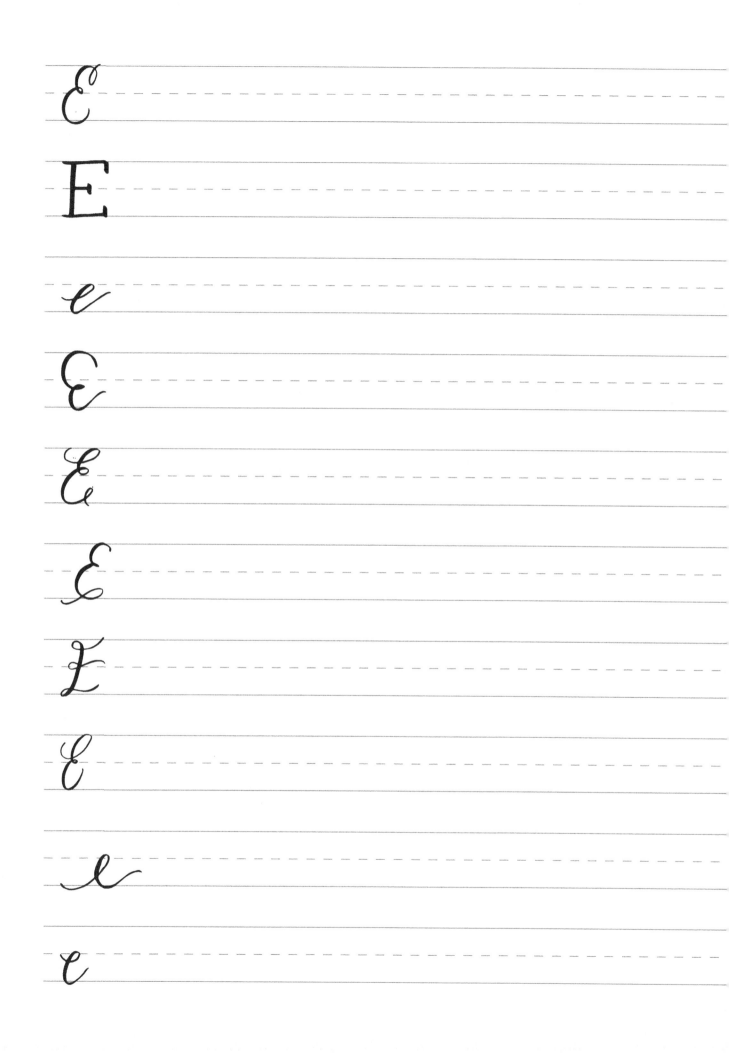

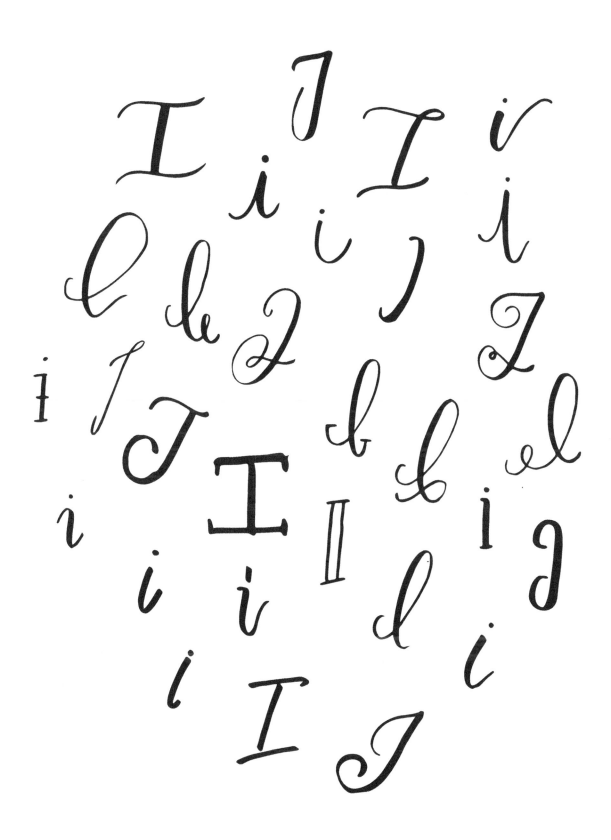

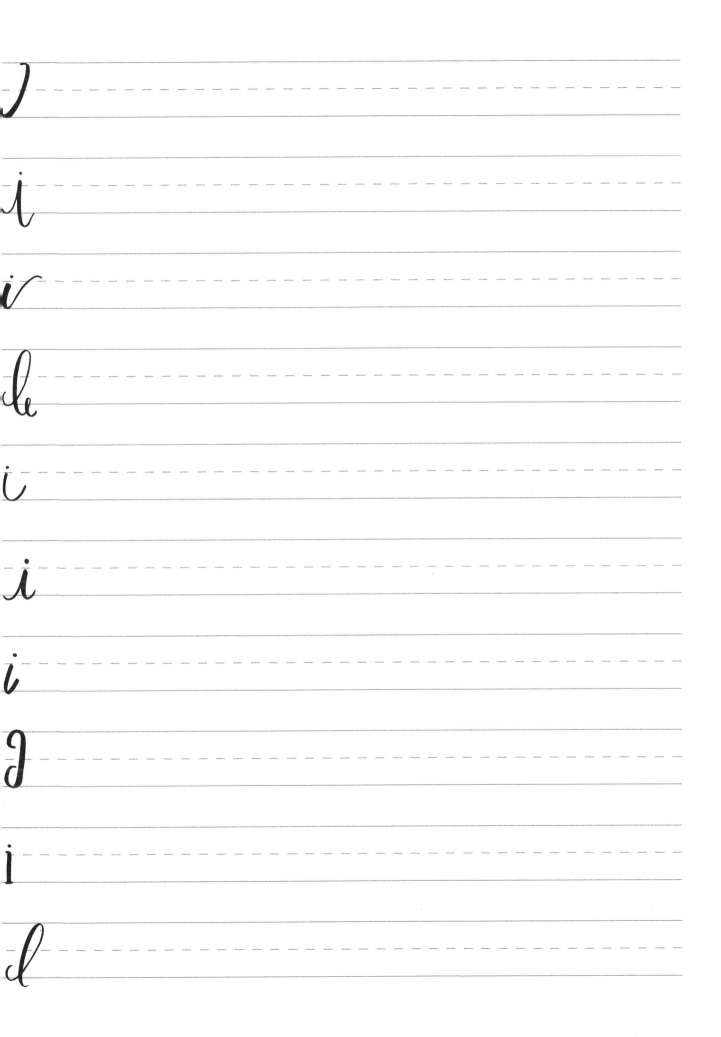

30 WAYS TO LETTER M

m

M

m

M

M

m

m

M

m

M

M M m m M m M M M M

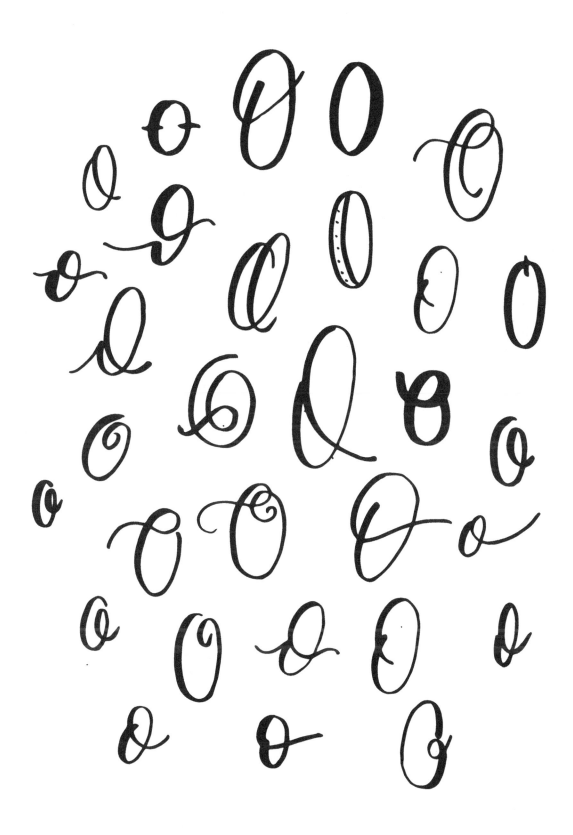

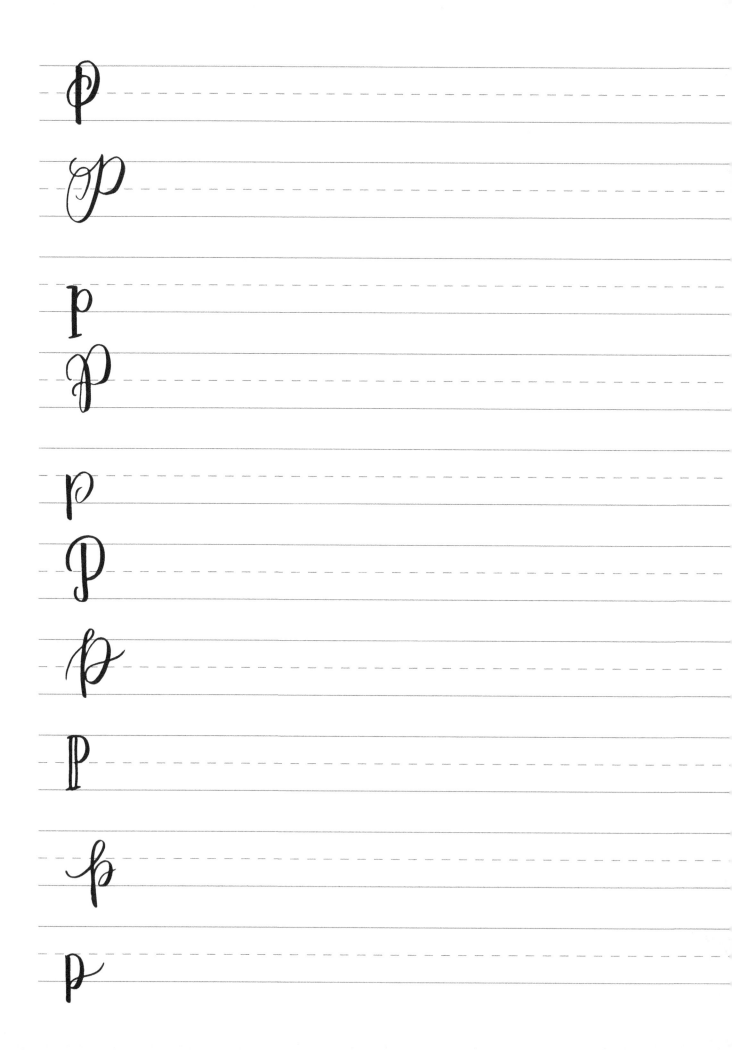

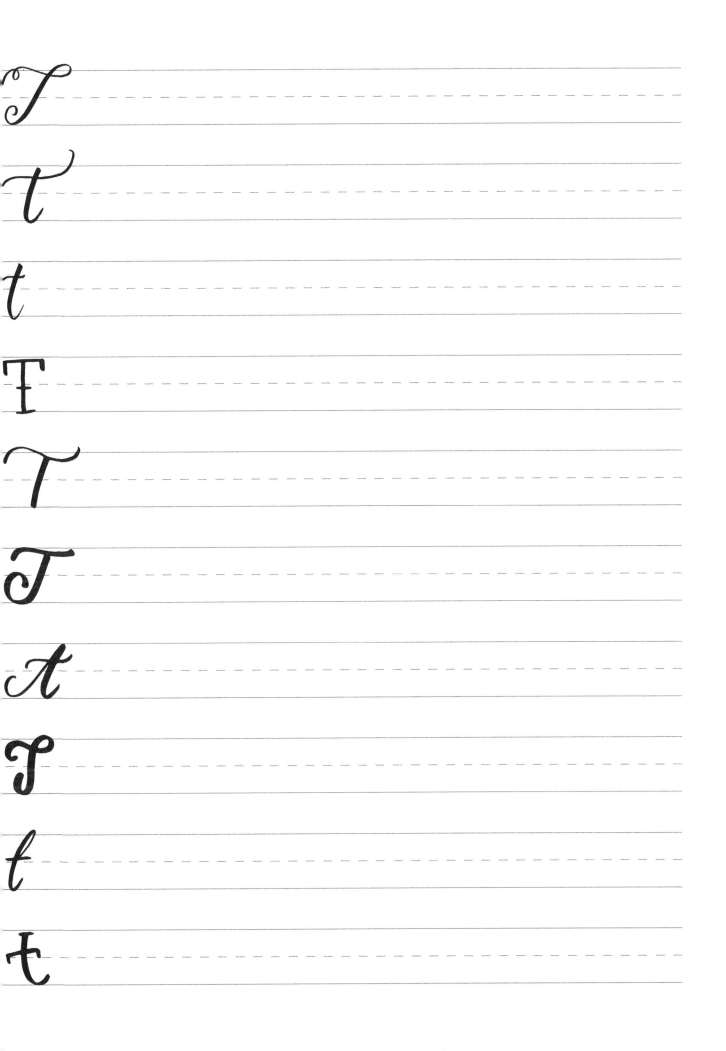

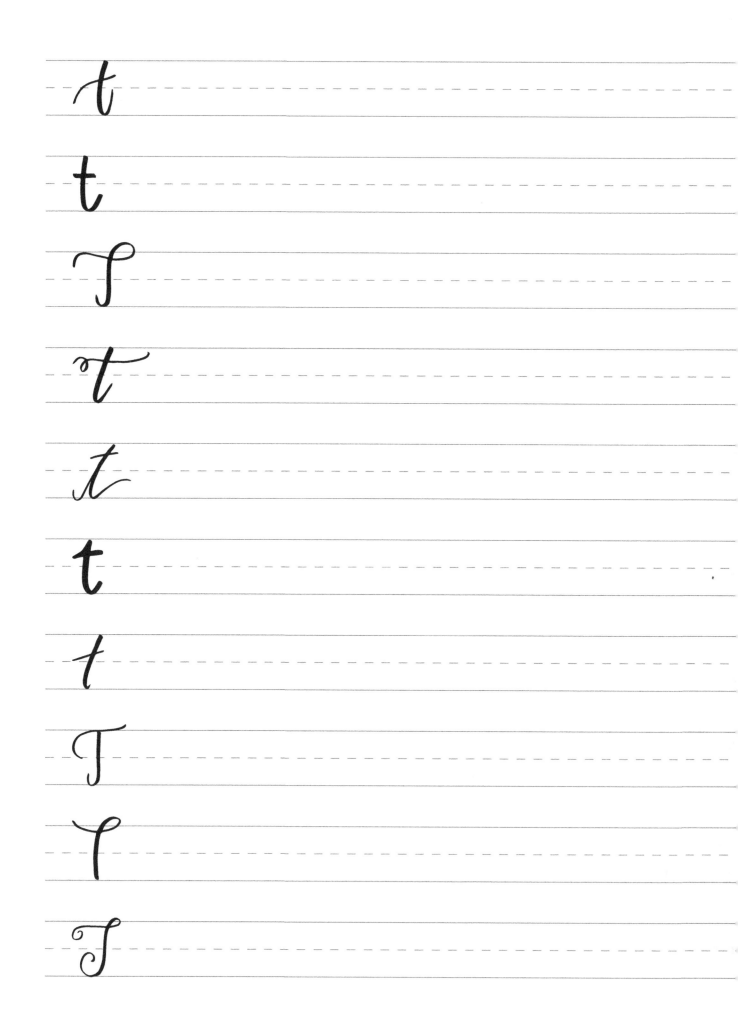

U

u

U

U

u

U

y

U

U

V

Uu

uo

y

U

U

eu

u

U

u

U

v

w

V

V

V

V

V

V

v

V

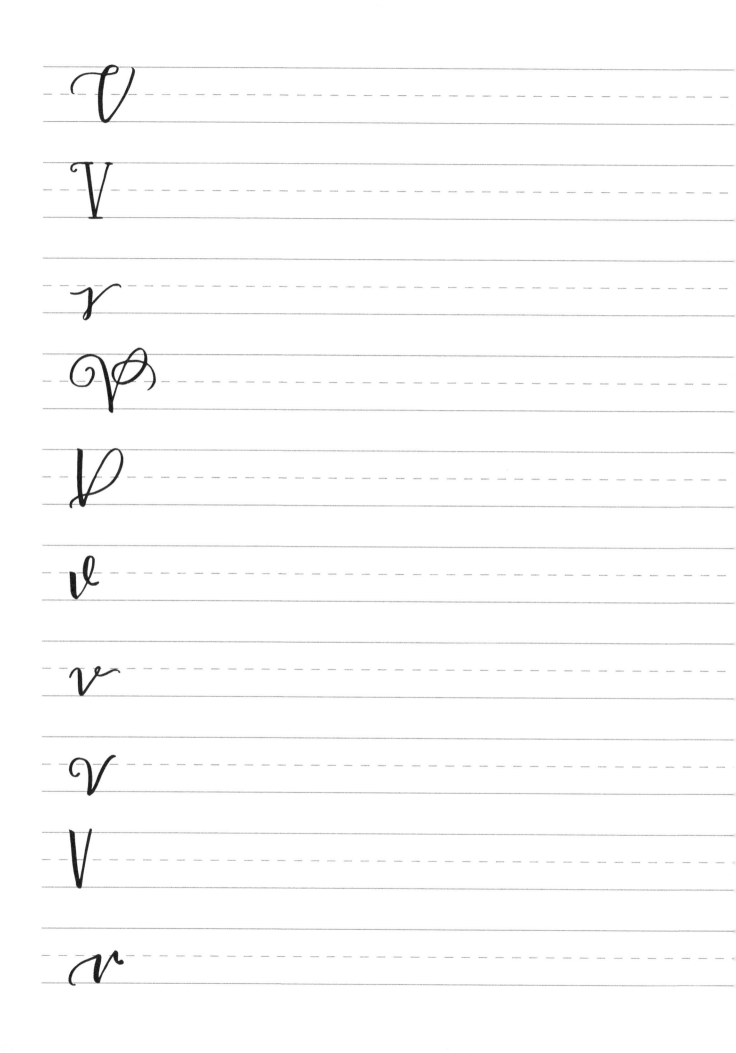

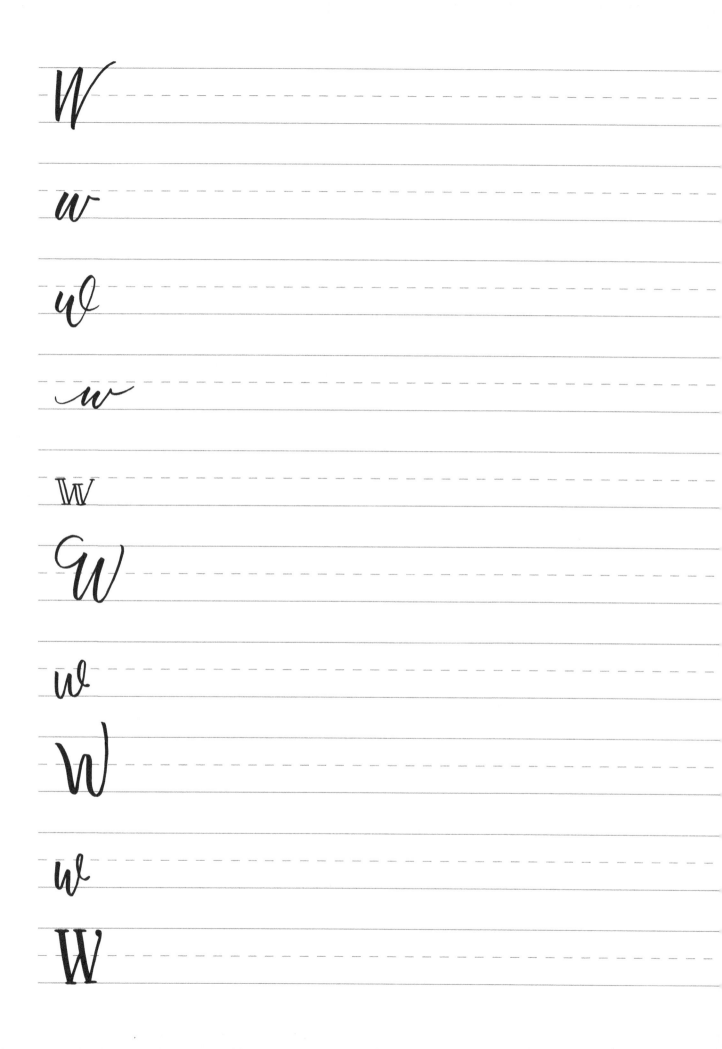

W

W

w

w

W

w

w

W

W

W

x

x

X

X

x

X

x

x

x

x

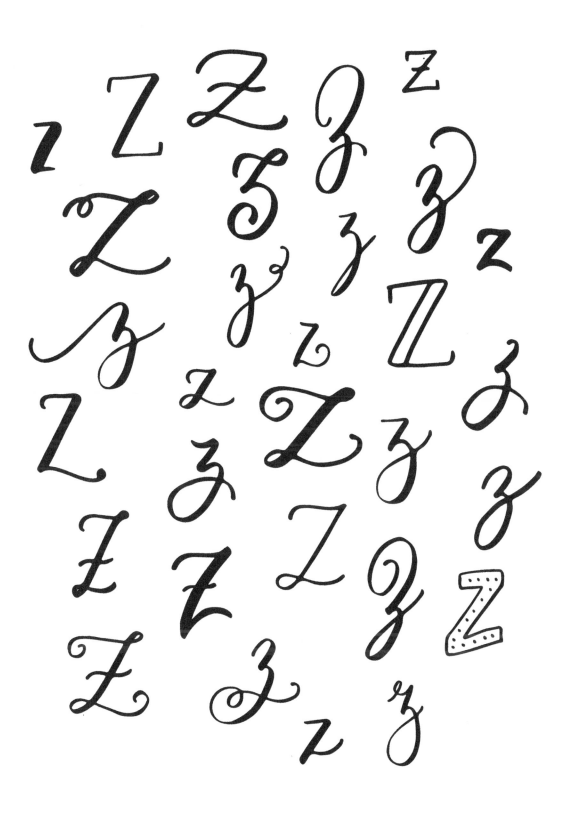

z

z

z

z

z

z

z

z

z

z

LETTERFORMS

A FEW GUIDELINES:

1. Try to stick to only two styles per design. This will help to create consistency and balance in your design. (You can go for three styles if you really feel it, but don't do more than 3!)

2. Try to create contrast between the two styles. A classic combination is a serif font paired with calligraphy.

3. Use different weights (thickness) to differentiate your styles.

4. Try not to pair two styles that are the same. For example, don't use two sans serif fonts. Mix a sans serif font with lettering or even a bold serif!

↓

The next few project pages give you some examples of how to combine different styles into one design!

Trace the light grey design and then try it on your own!

USE A MORE SIMPLE SAN SERIF STYLE TO FILL IN SPACE
BETWEEN TWO CALLIGRAPHY STYLES!

USE THE CURVES OF YOUR CALLIGRAPHY STYLE AS A
MOVING BASELINE FOR YOUR SERIF FONT!

MAKE
today
AMAZING

HAPPY
Birthday

MOLD THE LETTERS OF YOUR WORDS INTO A SHAPE, LIKE THIS CIRCLE DESIGN!

VARY THE ALIGNMENT IN YOUR DESIGN TO CREATE A MORE PLAYFUL FEEL!

let the

ADVENTURE

begin

Made in the USA
Monee, IL
01 July 2023